Noah's Ark

Adapted by Shawn South Aswad
Illustrated by Cheryl Mendenhall

Long, long ago there lived a very special man whose name was Noah. Noah was special because God chose him to do an important job.

One day God said to Noah, "I am not happy with the people on earth and have decided to send a great flood to cover the earth. I want you to build a huge boat. In this boat, I want you to carry your family and a pair of all living creatures, so that some may be saved."

Noah began to build the large boat which was called an ark. The ark was strong and sturdy, and it was made of gopher wood. It had one window and one door. When the ark was finished, Noah gathered together plenty of food. He needed to find enough food to feed his family and all the animals while they lived on the ark, because they would not see land for a long time.

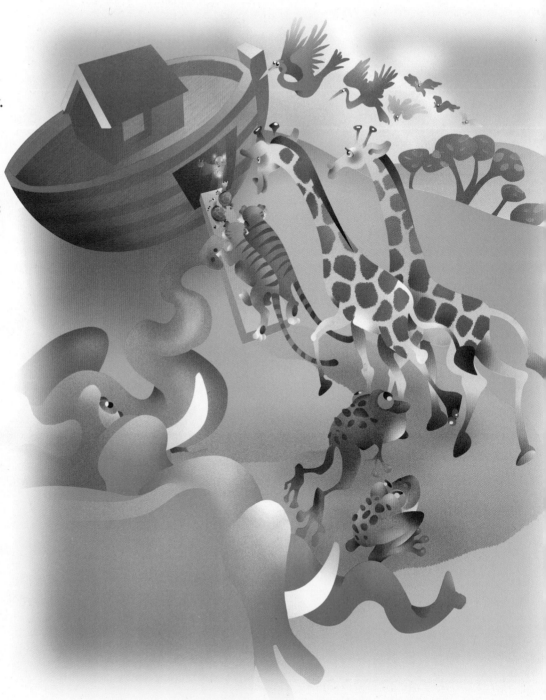

Finally he was ready, and Noah opened the door. Noah's wife and family entered the ark, and then the animals came in two by two. There were creatures of all kinds.

Noah had never seen so many animals.

The elephants did not look happy. "Don't worry," said Noah. "I have made the ark very large. There is plenty of room for everyone."

The birds
fluttered in fear.
"Don't worry,"
said Noah.
"I have
built the ark
very high so
you will be
able to fly."

The lions roared in anger. "Don't worry," said Noah. "I have gathered lots of food. There will be plenty for everyone to eat."

After every animal was safely on the ark, they heard a loud rumble. It was the sound of thunder… and then the rain began to fall. The rain poured down for forty days and forty nights. Water covered the earth, and Noah's ark rose high on the water.

After a while, the animals became grumpy. The birds were tired of being chased by the lions. The lions were tired of being pecked by the birds. The giraffes were just plain tired. All the animals were bored and ready to run free again.

One day, the ark hit something and came to a stop. It made a terrible ruckus. The giraffes fell on the zebras, the zebras fell on the lions, and the lions fell on the frogs. When everyone stood up again, they found themselves resting on top of a high mountain.

Noah sent a dove away from the ark to see if the land was dry. When the dove came back, Noah knew the earth was still under water. Noah sent out the dove a second time, and this time it brought back an olive branch. This was a sign that the dove had found dry land.

"Hooray!" exclaimed Noah. "The earth is dry again. We can all get off the ark!" The animals were excited and could hardly wait for Noah to open the door. When the door was opened, the animals rushed outside. The birds flew high in the sky while the snakes slithered low in the fresh grass.

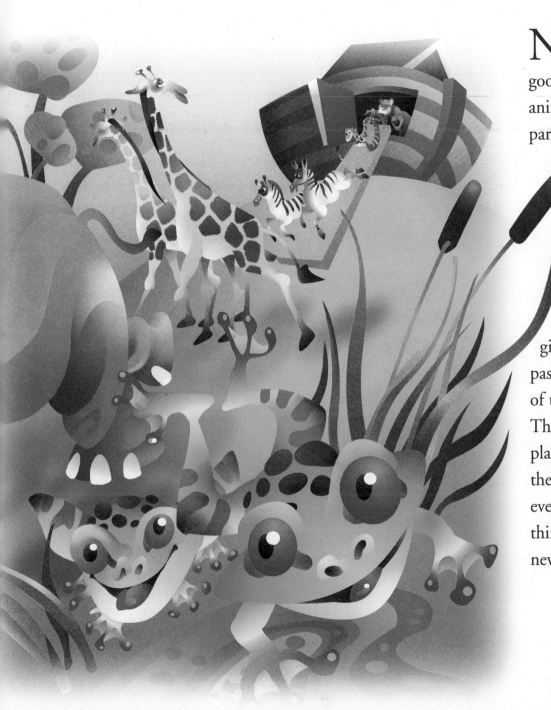

Noah said good-bye to the animals as they paraded off to find new homes. The elephants lumbered over the new land looking for food. The giraffes glided past in search of tall trees. The frogs hopped playfully toward the ponds. And every other living thing discovered a new place to live.

Noah and his family were happy with the work they had done for God. God spoke to Noah. "Noah," said God, "I am very pleased with your work, and I promise never to destroy the earth with water again. Look to the sky between the clouds for a sign of my promise and love." Noah looked up, and in the sky was the most beautiful thing he had ever seen. It was a rainbow full of bright colors.

So the next time it rains all day, and you think you will never go outside again, look for a rainbow. It is a sign of hope, and God's reminder that He will never destroy the earth by flood again.